DEC 2 8

The Science of
RENEWABLE
ENERGY

THE SCIENCE OF
SOLAR
ENERGY

by Arnold Ringstad

ReferencePoint
Press®

San Diego, CA

For more information, contact:
ReferencePoint Press, Inc.
PO Box 27779
San Diego, CA 92198
www.ReferencePointPress.com

Library of Congress Cataloging-in-Publication Data

Names: Ringstad, Arnold, author.
Title: The science of solar energy / by Arnold Ringstad.
Description: San Diego, CA : ReferencePoint Press, Inc., [2018] | Includes
    bibliographical references and index.
Identifiers: LCCN 2017042007| ISBN 9781682823071 (hardcover : alk. paper) |
    ISBN 9781682823088 (pdf)
Subjects: LCSH: Solar energy--Juvenile literature.
Classification: LCC TJ810.3 .R56 2018 | DDC 621.47--dc23
LC record available at https://lccn.loc.gov/2017042007

CONTENTS

IMPORTANT EVENTS IN THE
DEVELOPMENT OF SOLAR ENERGY   4

INTRODUCTION   6
Powered by Sunlight

CHAPTER 1   12
How Does Solar Power Work?

CHAPTER 2   28
Can Solar Power Replace Fossil Fuels?

CHAPTER 3   44
How Can Vehicles Use Solar Energy?

CHAPTER 4   58
What Is the Future of Solar Power?

Source Notes   72
For Further Research   76
Index   78
Image Credits   80
About the Author   80

IMPORTANT EVENTS IN THE DEVELOPMENT OF
SOLAR ENERGY

1958
The *Vanguard 1* satellite becomes the first space vehicle to use solar power.

1970s
Political conflicts over oil drive an interest in alternative energy sources, including solar power.

1950	1960	1970	1980	1990

1954
The modern history of photovoltaics begins as scientists demonstrate the first practical solar cell.

1987
The World Solar Challenge, a long-distance solar car race, begins in Australia.

1973
The University of Delaware builds Solar One, a home designed to demonstrate the potential of solar power.

1982
The 1-megawatt Arco Solar power plant in California opens.

1976
The first solar-powered calculator, the Sharp EL-8026, is released.

2009
Early research on using perovskite materials in solar cells begins.

2016
Entrepreneur Elon Musk announces plans for innovative solar roofing tiles.

2011
The *Juno* spacecraft departs for Jupiter on its way to becoming the most distant solar-powered spacecraft.

2005
The US Congress creates the Solar Investment Tax Credit (ITC) with the Energy Policy Act of 2005.

2015
The US Congress extends the Solar ITC through 2021.

2000	2005	2010	2015	2020

2012
The *PlanetSolar* ship completes the first around-the-world ocean voyage powered by solar cells.

2013
Construction begins on the Solar Star Projects, a massive photovoltaic solar power plant in California.

2016
The *Solar Impulse 2* aircraft completes the first around-the-world flight powered by solar cells.

2017
Automaker Toyota adds an option for a solar panel on the roof of some of its cars.

POWERED BY
SUNLIGHT

FROM THEORY TO APPLICATION

The Sun gives off vast amounts of energy. This energy travels outward in all directions as units of light called photons. Some of it hits Earth. People can harness the light as useful energy. There are two main methods for doing this. The first method is known as solar thermal power. The Sun's light warms the planet, and solar thermal power involves using this heat. Some types of solar thermal power use the heat directly, creating hot water for homes and businesses. Other types use this heat to make steam, which can power a turbine and generate electricity. The second method uses **photovoltaic** cells. These devices are made up of layers of **silicon** or other materials. The materials are designed so that when they are struck by photons, electricity flows through them. This electricity can be captured and put to use.

North of Los Angeles, California, lies sun-drenched Antelope Valley. This basin, named for the pronghorns that once leapt across its dusty scrubland, covers 3,000 square miles (7,800 sq km). In the past, the area was home to a small number of farms. Seen from above, small patches of green fields dotted the dry, brown landscape.

But in recent years, something new has risen from the soil of Antelope Valley. Glassy blue panels have appeared in angular parcels along the basin floor. The transmission lines and other electrical infrastructure nearby reveal what is going on. The millions of panels here make up photovoltaic (PV) solar power plants. These installations generate vast amounts of electricity using the valley's abundant sunlight. The largest of Antelope Valley's solar power plants—and at the time of its construction, the largest in the world—is the Solar Star Projects.

The Solar Star Projects consist of two parts, Solar Star 1 and Solar Star 2, located next to each other a few miles west of Rosamond, California. Construction on this huge installation began in early 2013. Over the next two years, workers set up more than 1.7 million panels, covering 3,200 acres (1,300 ha). Together, the Solar Star Projects are able to generate some 586 megawatts of electricity, enough to power about 255,000 typical American homes. According to the California Energy Commission, "The Solar Star projects generate enough electricity to displace approximately 570,000 tons [517,100 metric t] of carbon dioxide per year—the equivalent of taking nearly 108,000 cars off the road annually."[1]

Besides incorporating advanced solar panels, the power plant would take advantage of other technologies to keep

A robot cleans dust and other debris off of solar panels at the Atacama Solar Plant in Chile. A similar technology helps keep panels in the Solar Star Projects clean so that sunlight can easily filter through.

efficiency up, lower costs, and be friendlier to the environment. When solar panels are covered in dust or debris, some of the sunlight is blocked and their power output drops. Keeping panels clean is an important part of maintaining these plants. But ordinary cleaning processes are time-consuming and use a lot of water. The developers of the Solar Star Projects instead decided to use cleaning robots to keep the vast rows of panels dust-free. The robots slide along the panels, washing them as they go. The process uses 75 percent less water than hand-cleaning would. Even better, the robots get the job done ten times faster than the old method.

The builders finished their work in 2015, and on July 1, the power plant went fully online. Experts in the industry recognized it as both a turning point in the solar industry and a telltale sign of a continuing trend in solar's rising importance. Cory Honeyman, a solar analyst at clean energy study group GTM Research, said, "Solar Star's completion is a milestone for the US and global solar markets. It provides yet another proof of concept that mega-scale solar farms can be achieved ahead of schedule."[2]

The State of Solar Today

Enormous solar power plants like the Solar Star Projects represent just one sector of the solar power industry. Elsewhere in the world of photovoltaics, smaller **arrays** of panels turn light into electricity on the roofs of businesses and homes. Ultra-efficient vehicles on land, in the air, at sea, and even in space use PV panels for power. Tiny PV cells even power devices such as calculators and wristwatches.

> **WORDS IN CONTEXT**
>
> **arrays**
> Groupings of multiple panels.

The industry also includes solar thermal technologies, which harness the Sun's heat. On the small scale, solar water heaters provide hot water for individual homes. Large-scale thermal systems are known as concentrating solar power (CSP). In CSP, mirrors or lenses focus sunlight onto a small point, heating up that point to extremely high temperatures. That heat is used to boil water into steam, and that steam spins a turbine to generate electricity.

While both PV and thermal technologies show promise, and both are in use today, a 2015 study by the Massachusetts Institute of Technology (MIT) predicted that PV would "continue for some time to be the main source of solar generation in the United States."[3] The key reason for this is cost. For large installations in sunny regions, PV is about 25 percent cheaper than CSP. In cloudier areas, where CSP loses more effectiveness than PV, the price of PV can be up to 50 percent cheaper.

The Dawn of the Solar Era?

The price advantage of PV is not limited only to a comparison against CSP. The prices of solar cells dropped dramatically in the 2010s, falling as much as 12 percent in 2015 alone. The result is that PV is becoming cheap not only compared with other **renewable** energy sources, but also compared with traditional fossil fuels. According to a 2017 report by Bloomberg New Energy Finance, solar energy "will be cheaper than coal in China, India, Mexico, the U.K. [United Kingdom] and Brazil" by 2021.[4] Fossil fuels are nonrenewable, and using them spews pollutants into the atmosphere that can harm both human health and the environment. By contrast, solar cells generate no pollution while operating.

> **WORDS IN CONTEXT**
>
> **renewable**
> Something that is not depleted when it is used.

While price and cleanliness present advantages, solar power also faces challenges. The most obvious issue is that the Sun isn't always shining. In cloudy conditions, the available sunlight drops significantly, and at night there isn't sunlight. To make power available at all times, people must either store the electricity generated by solar systems to use when the Sun isn't shining or rely upon other sources of energy. Challenges also exist in connecting solar power systems to existing electrical grids. And along the way, future government policies may either help or hinder the expansion of the solar industry.

If solar power's promise pays off, it may become a major power source in the twenty-first century. Gregory Wilson of the US Department of Energy's (DOE's) National Center for Photovoltaics sees the combination of low prices and environmental friendliness as key to solar's success: "The ultimate point of all of this is that PV is quickly positioning itself to be a really big player in the world. For anyone who cares about climate change and carbon **emissions**, but who also cares about quality of life and not upending the economy, it is going to be a very desirable thing."[5]

WORDS IN CONTEXT

emissions
Something, such as gas, that is given off from a source.

HOW DOES
SOLAR POWER WORK?

Solar energy is perhaps the most direct way by which people harness the power of sunlight. PV panels turn that light into electricity, and solar thermal systems make use of the Sun's heat. But these are not the only energy sources that originate with the Sun. In fact, nearly all of the energy we use ultimately comes from the Sun. The Sun's heat creates Earth's weather patterns, making the breezes that spin wind turbines. Its energy also drives the water cycle, creating the fast-flowing rivers that power hydroelectric plants. Even fossil fuels, formed when the remains of ancient plants were compressed over millions of years, received their original energy input from the Sun. In the process of **photosynthesis**, those ancient plants took in sunlight to keep themselves alive. When fossil fuels are burned today, that same energy is being released. So, studying the Sun

WORDS IN CONTEXT

photosynthesis

The process by which plants take in carbon dioxide, water, and sunlight and use them to produce oxygen and food.

is important to understanding not only solar power, but also nearly all human energy use.

Solar Science

The Sun is a star. It is one of hundreds of billions of stars in our galaxy. The Sun dominates its nearby area, known as the solar system. Eight planets—including Earth—and thousands of smaller objects, such as asteroids and comets, orbit the Sun. The Sun has a mass more than seven hundred times greater than that of all the planets combined.

The Sun's enormous mass means that it has extremely strong gravity, and the force of this gravity pulls the Sun's mass inward. The result is a very hot, dense object. At the Sun's core, temperatures reach at least 27 million°F (15 million°C). These extreme conditions make it possible for a reaction called nuclear fusion to occur. In nuclear fusion, hydrogen atoms smash against each other, combining to form helium atoms. The new helium atom has a smaller mass than the individual hydrogen atoms did, and this extra mass is released as energy. The Sun is made up of about 90 percent hydrogen, providing enough fuel to power its fusion for billions of years into the future.

Some of the energy released by the fusion process comes in the form of photons, or individual units of light. They travel outward from the Sun's core, but the extreme density within the Sun means that the photons can travel only a few millimeters before colliding with an atom. When this happens, they may be absorbed and emitted again. This occurs repeatedly, with the photons taking what scientists call a "random walk" from the core to the surface. It typically takes a photon about 170,000 years to complete this process.

Once photons reach the Sun's surface, they zip outward in all directions through space at the speed of light. The speed of light is approximately 186,200 miles per second (299,660 km/sec). It takes about eight minutes for the photons to cross the 93 million miles (150 million km) between the Sun and Earth. The streams of photons that reach Earth provide the planet with daylight. When this light strikes the planet's surface, its energy is released as heat. The ground radiates this heat into the atmosphere, warming the planet and keeping it habitable for life. The light and warmth provided by the Sun make solar power possible.

Thermal Solar Power: Using the Sun's Heat

People have been taking advantage of the Sun's heat to control temperatures in buildings for thousands of years. By building houses in a particular orientation with respect to the Sun's position in the sky, architects could warm homes in winter and cool them in the summer. The ancient Greek philosopher Socrates noted that "in houses that look toward the south, the Sun penetrates the portico in winter, while in summer the path of the Sun is right over our heads, and above the roof, so that there is shade."[6] Other ancient civilizations, including the Pueblo Indian tribes of North America, made similar observations and applied these lessons to their construction. In modern times, people still design buildings with this in mind. They also use two newer methods of harnessing the Sun's heat energy: flat-plate collectors and concentrating collectors.

Flat-plate collectors are typically made up of a dark layer of metal covered by sheets of glass. When sunlight shines upon the collector, the metal heats up. The glass helps prevent reflected light from escaping, keeping the metal plate warm. Behind the plate, water or air flows in tubes, and the heat from the metal is transferred to this fluid. The hot water can then be stored in an insulated tank for later use in bathing, dishwashing, and other household applications. The hot fluid may also be sent through pipes in floors or ceilings, heating a building. Water or air in flat-plate collectors is generally heated to around 200°F (93°C).

Whereas flat-plate collectors use sunlight directly, concentrating collectors focus the Sun's rays to achieve dramatically higher temperatures. These systems are generally used in power plants rather than for individual homes. Mirrors or lenses are shaped and arranged to direct light onto a small target, such as a dark-colored pipe with fluid running through it or a material that can absorb and retain heat. Dark colors are used because they absorb more of the Sun's energy than light colors. The high-intensity light can heat its target to temperatures of 3,600°F (2,000°C). This heat is then used to boil water into steam, which spins a turbine to produce electricity.

Concentrating collectors have a key advantage over flat-plate collectors: some types of concentrating collectors can continue generating electricity at night. In concentrating collector power plants,

In a concentrating collector system, mirrors reflect light onto a fluid-filled pipe. Concentrating collectors at the Solar Energy Systems plant in California's Mojave Desert focus sunlight onto tubes filled with oil.

materials known as molten salts can be used as the target of the focused sunlight. Molten salts can remain hot for hours, retaining the heat they absorbed and releasing it slowly over time. This means that they can continue to create steam and generate electricity at night, after the Sun drops below the horizon.

Applications of Thermal Solar Power

One common use of thermal solar power is in home water heating. Traditional water heaters run on fossil fuels or electricity. Using a system powered by free sunlight can save consumers money. There are two basic types of solar water heaters: active and passive. In active systems, pumps circulate water through the collector device. In passive systems, no outside energy source is needed to move water through the system. The DOE reports that passive systems "are typically less expensive than active systems, but they're usually not as efficient."[7] Within each of these two categories, there are multiple designs that use various configurations of collectors, pipes, and tanks. Specific types of systems are better suited for particular climates.

Solar water heating is also done on a larger scale. One such installation can be seen at Burj Khalifa, the world's tallest skyscraper. This towering structure, completed in 2009, rises 2,716 feet (828 m) above the coastal city of Dubai, United Arab Emirates. The building's designers recognized that an essential part of any modern structure is energy efficiency and sustainability. Ahmad Al Matrooshi, a managing director with the building's development company, noted that "energy efficient measures . . . are not an option but an imperative for sustainable growth."[8] The building's 378 solar collectors each measure 29 square feet (2.7 sq m) in area. Together, they are capable of heating up 37,000 gallons (140,000 L) of water using seven hours of sunshine. This hot water is then piped to businesses and apartments elsewhere in the building.

While solar water heaters come in sizes both large and small, concentrating solar power installations have generally been built only at power-plant scale. These large power stations are significantly more complex than solar water heaters. CSP engineers must design and arrange a series of mirrors or lenses, select materials that can handle extreme temperatures, and find a way to efficiently turn that heat into electricity. CSP plants typically have a generating capacity of 100 megawatts or more.

The Ivanpah Solar Plant in California is an example of one of these CSP installations. It is located at Ivanpah Lake, a dry lakebed in the Mojave Desert near the Nevada border. The Ivanpah plant uses a power tower system. In this CSP plant design, a central tower has a solar receiver and boiler at its top. It is surrounded by concentric circles of mirrors on the ground that all reflect light onto this receiver. The mirrors, known as heliostats, are mounted on devices that tilt them so that they can track the Sun as it moves through the sky. The extreme intensity of the light at the receiver heats it up to very high temperatures, which the boiler uses to create superheated steam. This steam is then piped down the tower to a turbine, where it generates electricity.

The Ivanpah plant has three separate towers. Each is 459 feet (140 m) tall, and each is surrounded by its own set of heliostat mirrors. In all, the Ivanpah plant has approximately 300,000 of these heliostats. The entire installation covers some 3,500 acres (1,400 ha). Together, the three towers generate about 377 megawatts of electricity.

Thousands of heliostat mirrors reflect light onto a central tower in California's Ivanpah Solar Plant. This solar plant was completed and connected to the electrical grid in 2013.

The project's developer, BrightSource, says that this is "enough to serve more than 140,000 homes in California during the peak hours of the day."[9]

Photovoltaic Cells: Using the Sun's Light

Photovoltaic cells offer another way to turn the Sun's energy into electricity. Rather than using sunlight's heat, photovoltaics use the sunlight itself. The modern history of this technology dates back to 1954. In that year, scientists with New Jersey's Bell Labs demonstrated the first practical solar cell. It was similar in appearance to modern solar cells, but it was primitive by today's standards. This experimental silicon device was used to power a small radio transmitter. The *New York Times* reported that the silicon solar cell "may mark the beginning of a new era."[10] Over the next few decades, PV cells remained much too expensive for ordinary consumers, but they found widespread use in satellites.

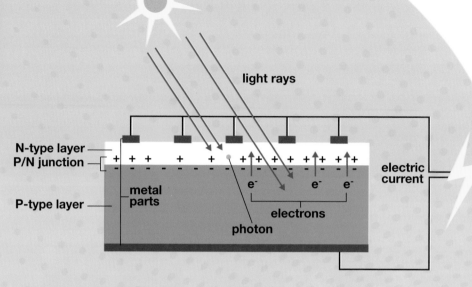

N-type layer
P/N junction

metal parts

P-type layer

light rays

e⁻   e⁻   e⁻

electric current

electrons

photon

Inside a Photovoltaic Cell

PV cells have improved a great deal over the past few decades, but the basic scientific principles behind them remain the same. A solar cell contains two layers of semiconducting materials, most commonly silicon. One layer, called the N-type layer, contains extra electrons. The other layer, called the P-type layer, contains extra empty spaces where electrons can go. The place where the layers meet is known as the P/N junction.

When a photon hits the solar cell, it may knock one of the electrons free. Both the electron and the empty space, or hole, it left behind can then move around the cell. The electron is drawn to the N-type layer, and the hole is drawn to the P-type layer. The moving electrons create an electric current. Metal parts conduct this electricity, carrying it away for use or storage before returning the electrons to the cell.

In the 1970s, political conflicts over oil, one of the world's leading fossil fuels, led to renewed investment in other energy sources, including solar power. PV technology improved over time, dropping in price and converting more of the Sun's energy into useful electricity. Solar cells appeared in small devices, such as watches and calculators. They also appeared in larger sizes as panels on the roofs of homes and businesses. Eventually, they were collected in power plants as huge solar arrays. According to the nonprofit environmental organization the Earth Policy Institute, "The price of solar photovoltaic panels has declined . . . from $74 a watt in 1972 to less than 70 cents a watt in 2014."[11]

Energy, Bandgaps, and Efficiency

Each photon that strikes a solar cell has a particular amount of energy, measured in units called electron volts (eV). The energy varies based on where the photon falls on the electromagnetic spectrum. For example, the energy of photons in the visible light range of the spectrum ranges from 1.65 eV to 3.1 eV. Some kinds of photons, such as those that make up radio waves, have less energy. Others, such as those that make up X-rays, have more energy. About 50 percent of the energy in sunlight is made up of visible light. An additional 40 percent consists of lower-energy photons, and the final 10 percent consists of higher-energy photons.

Inside a solar cell, the amount of energy needed to knock an electron loose is known as the bandgap. The value of the bandgap varies based on the materials used to construct the cell. In the case of silicon solar cells, the bandgap is 1.1 eV. When a photon with lower energy than the bandgap strikes the cell, it is unable to knock

Multijunction Solar Cells

Though traditional silicon solar cells theoretically top out at an efficiency of about 33 percent, there is a way to get efficiency even higher: multijunction cells. Traditional cells have one silicon P/N junction that can be used to generate electricity. In multijunction cells, several layers of different materials meet at multiple junctions. The top layer has a high bandgap, capturing high-energy photons and letting lower-energy ones pass through. The next layer down has a lower bandgap, and a third layer has a still lower bandgap. This design, with multiple bandgaps and multiple junctions, allows the cell to turn more of the sunlight's energy into electricity. Scientists have demonstrated efficiencies as high as 45 percent with this technology.

Rather than using silicon, multijunction solar cells are made out of different semiconductor materials, such as gallium indium phosphate and gallium arsenide. Complex manufacturing methods are needed to assemble multijunction cells. These materials and production techniques make multijunction cells much too expensive for everyday use. They have mostly been reserved for use in satellites and other spacecraft. In these applications, generating the most electricity possible for a given weight of solar cells is important, and high cost is usually not a barrier. However, researchers are investigating ways to drive down costs and make multijunction cells more widely accessible.

an electron loose. Instead, it simply warms the solar panel slightly. When a photon with higher energy than the bandgap hits the cell, it successfully knocks an electron loose. However, the photon's additional energy beyond the bandgap is not captured. Because their energy is greater than 1.1 eV, the photons in visible light, with energies ranging from 1.65 eV to 3.1 eV, can always knock an electron loose in a silicon solar cell. But this also means that any extra energy beyond the bandgap is wasted.

This wasted energy reduces the solar cell's efficiency. The DOE defines this efficiency as "the percentage of the solar energy shining on a PV device that is converted into usable electricity."[12] Of all the solar energy hitting a typical silicon PV panel, about 18 percent is lost because it has less energy than the bandgap. Another 49 percent is lost as excess energy in photons with a greater energy than the bandgap. That leaves 33 percent. In theory, this is the maximum efficiency of a silicon solar cell.

In addition to the bandgap issue, other factors can reduce the efficiency of solar cells. One is a process called recombination, which comes in two types: direct and indirect. In direct recombination, a freed electron and a hole run into each other before flowing through the cell as electrical current, combining and emitting a photon rather than generating electricity. In indirect recombination, electrons or holes run into an impurity or defect in the solar cell material and release their energy as heat. Another factor affecting efficiency is temperature. High temperatures can change the properties of the silicon, reducing the amount of electricity generated. The solar cell material's reflectivity can impact efficiency, too. Silicon is a naturally reflective substance, reflecting more than 30 percent of the light that hits it. Solar cell designers use antireflective coatings and textured surfaces to reduce this number, keeping more of the sunlight (and its energy) in the cell. These special coatings are what give solar cells their familiar black or dark blue appearance.

Thin-film solar cells are an alternative to silicon cells. These use different materials, such as cadmium telluride. Unlike traditional panels, thin-film solar cells are flexible. Their flexibility allows them to be mounted on curved surfaces or rolled up for storage. Historically, thin-film cells have been cheaper than silicon-based ones, but their efficiency has also been lower. However, major advances have been made in recent years, and the efficiency of thin-film designs has improved dramatically.

Applications of Photovoltaic Cells

Photovoltaic cells have a wide range of uses, from providing the electricity to run a single, small device to generating power for an entire community. On the smallest end of this scale, they have been a part of wristwatches and calculators since the 1970s. Solar watches feature tiny cells on their faces that charge a small battery within the watch. The cells on some early versions were prominent, driving some fashion-conscious consumers away. However, modern solar watches are often almost indistinguishable from other types. Solar-powered calculators have also become more practical over time. The very first model, the Sharp EL-8026, came out in 1976. Its solar panels were on the back, meaning that users had to let the calculator sit face-down in the Sun to charge before using it. Later calculators moved their smaller, more efficient cells to the front of the device. Solar watches and calculators both remain popular today.

On a larger scale, photovoltaic cells have found widespread use in home solar power installations. The history of solar power at the household level dates back to 1973, when the University of Delaware built Solar One, a prototype home designed to showcase the potential of thermal and photovoltaic solar technologies. Karl Böer, who led the project, described it in a 1973 research paper: "The roof contains 24 panels, which may be replaced at ease."[13] It wasn't until the 1990s, however, that a combination of falling panel costs and new government tax incentives started to make photovoltaics an attractive option for homeowners.

Individual solar cells produce small amounts of electricity, so home solar installations typically use solar panels, which are made up of multiple cells. Depending on their size and efficiency, panels "range in output from 10–300 watts" each, according to the DOE.[14] Home solar installations generally take the form of an array mounted on the roof.

In addition to the solar cells themselves, solar panels have several other components. The top surface of the panel is typically covered in glass, which allows light through while also protecting the cell from weather. Behind the cell is the rear surface, often made of a sheet of a durable plastic material known as polyvinyl fluoride. It keeps the cell sealed away from water and gases. Holding the top surface, cell, and rear surface together is an encapsulant, commonly made up of sheets of a flexible plastic material called ethyl vinyl acetate. Finally, an aluminum structure frames the panel.

Home solar installations also require additional equipment. Mounting racks hold the panels securely in place on the rooftop. Wiring carries the generated electricity from the panels into the house. A device called an inverter turns the panels' electricity from a form called direct current (DC) to a form called alternating current (AC), which is preferred for household use. From there, the power can either be used right away or stored in batteries for later.

Measuring Power and Energy

When discussing the generation of electricity, it's important to understand the concepts of power and energy, as well as the units in which they are measured. Power describes how much electricity is being used or generated at a given moment. It is measured in watts. This unit is named in honor of Scottish inventor James Watt, who improved steam engine technology in the late eighteenth century. Energy describes how much electricity is being used over time. It is measured in watt-hours. For example, a 10-watt light bulb draws 10 watts of power when it is turned on. If it is left on for one hour, it has used 10 watt-hours of energy.

Larger amounts of power and energy can be described using the metric prefixes kilo-, mega-, and giga-. The power used by a household might be measured in kilowatts, or thousands of watts. The power generated by a power plant could be measured in megawatts, or millions of watts. The power used by a large city may be described in gigawatts, or billions of watts.

Utility-scale solar PV power plants, such as the Solar Star Projects, represent the largest-scale use of solar cells to generate electricity. One early solar PV plant, built by Arco Solar in California in 1982, had a generating capacity of about 1 megawatt, enough to power hundreds of homes. Its 108 panels covered an area of about 20 acres (8 ha). Over the next few decades, PV plants grew bigger, but they still generated much less power than their fossil fuel counterparts. By 2009, the largest solar power plant in the United States was the one at Nellis Air Force Base near Las Vegas, Nevada, with a capacity of 14 megawatts. By comparison, the largest coal and nuclear power plants have capacities of more than 1 gigawatt, or 1,000 megawatts.

The world of utility-scale solar power changed dramatically over the next few years. A combination of improving technology, decreasing costs, and government incentives, such as loan programs, boosted the size of solar power plants around the world. The Solar Star Projects were the world's largest solar PV facility upon their completion in 2015, but even then, larger ones were in the works. In September 2016, an enormous new solar power plant opened in Tamil Nadu, India. Made up of 2.5 million panels covering about 2,500 acres (1,000 ha), the station has a generating capacity of approximately 648 megawatts. The BBC reported that this power plant "is estimated to make enough power for 750,000 people."[15] Multiple PV power plants with capacities well over 100 megawatts can now be found in the United States, India, China, and elsewhere. Utility-scale solar power has become a key source of power in communities across the globe.

CAN SOLAR POWER
REPLACE FOSSIL FUELS?

For the last few centuries, most of the world's power has been supplied by fossil fuels. These substances are the carbon-rich remains of ancient plants and animals. Over millions of years, these remains **decomposed** and were put under immense pressure and heat as they were buried under layers of rock and sediment.

Eventually, this process formed the fossil fuels we find underground today. Fossil fuels are known as nonrenewable resources because they take so long to create and are a limited resource in the scale of a human lifetime.

Widespread use of fossil fuels began in the eighteenth century, when scientists and inventors found ways to burn them to generate energy. The fuels proved useful in factories, in generating electricity, and in powering vehicle engines. By the early twenty-first century, fossil fuels provided about 90 percent of the energy used by developed nations. Is it possible for solar power to disrupt the dominance of fossil fuels? To answer this question, it is important to understand the major fossil fuels, their strengths and weaknesses, and the potential advantages and disadvantages of solar energy. The three most significant fossil fuels are coal, oil, and natural gas.

Coal, a brown or black solid material, is found in layers of rock. Miners travel underground to find and extract it. When burned, coal releases heat that can be used to drive a turbine and generate electricity. It can also be turned into a liquid form. Coal rose to prominence in the early eighteenth century, when people found it was useful in the iron production process. In the late eighteenth century, it received another boost when inventor James Watt developed a steam engine that could use the heat of burning coal. Today, coal-fueled power plants are a major source of US electricity.

Oil is a fossil fuel found underground in liquid form. People dig wells to extract it from underground reservoirs. The oil is taken to a refinery, where it is turned into a variety of products, including heating oil, asphalt, and the gasoline and diesel fuels used in cars and trucks. The oil industry expanded dramatically after the introduction of the automobile in the early twentieth century. Oil is typically measured in units called barrels. One barrel is equal to 42 gallons (159 L). The oil industry processes more than 80 million barrels of oil each day.

Natural gas is a colorless, odorless gas that is often found dissolved in oil deposits. It is commonly used as a fuel to heat homes, though it has also become a major fuel source for power plants. Ancient civilizations going back thousands of years, including those in Iran and China, were familiar with deposits of natural gas and made some use of this resource. But until the twentieth century, the lack of a reliable way to transport natural gas over long distances limited its popularity. The late 1920s brought new pipeline technology, and over the course of the next several decades, countries built thousands of miles of new pipes to carry natural gas to homes and businesses.

These fossil fuels remain popular for several reasons. They have major advantages over competing energy sources, including renewable ones. For one thing, though there is a limited supply of fossil fuels, they have been relatively plentiful up to this time. They have also been inexpensive to extract, process, and distribute. Because the world has been running on fossil fuels for so long, scientists and engineers are extremely familiar with them, and a huge amount of **infrastructure** has been designed with them in mind. Finally, fossil fuels are extremely energy-dense. They pack a lot of energy into a relatively small mass and volume, making them highly useful for transportation, where the available space for fuel tanks is limited.

By 2016, coal, oil, and natural gas dominated energy production in the United States and worldwide. The US Energy Information Administration reported that "about 65%" of the electricity generated in the United States that year came from fossil fuels "and about 15% was from renewable energy sources."[16] Less than 1 percent of electricity came from solar power.

It's clear that solar energy has a long way to go to challenge the established fossil fuels. However, fossil fuels have many problems that are leading people to seek alternate energy sources, including solar. Additionally, solar power possesses many distinct advantages over fossil fuels. Though it also introduces some new challenges, researchers are finding ways to overcome these issues to make solar energy more attractive. Another key factor in the rise of solar power will be government policies supporting it. Already, government incentives have helped the solar industry grow dramatically in recent years. Continued support could help solar power become a more significant source of energy and play a role in replacing the world's use of fossil fuels.

Fossil Fuel Problems and Solar Benefits

The beneficial aspects of fossil fuels, including their widespread availability, low cost, and high energy density, have made them the world's primary energy source over the last century. But they also have significant downsides. Some of these problems have been recognized since the earliest days of fossil fuel use. Other issues have only become apparent to modern science more recently.

Coal mining has always been hazardous to workers. The ceilings of mines can cave in, crushing miners or trapping them deep below the surface. The coal extraction process can release flammable

Workers place a floating containment barrier off the coast of California in the Pacific Ocean after a 2015 oil spill. Cleaning up oil spills is dangerous and can lead to health problems such as respiratory issues.

gases, creating a risk of mine explosions. And even when the mining goes successfully, breathing in coal dust over the course of a career in the mines can cause severe respiratory conditions known collectively as black lung disease. Even today, with improved safety standards in many parts of the world, hundreds of coal miners around the world die or are injured on the job each year. In 2017, the International Labour Organization reported that "in most countries, mining remains the most hazardous occupation."[17]

By contrast, the solar energy industry is much safer for its workers. Employees in facilities that produce solar cells and panels face the usual safety concerns that apply to any factory setting. Workers who install panels must contend with the normal safety issues that accompany construction projects, such as falls, electrical hazards, and potentially dangerous heavy machinery. Government regulations and industry practices aim to minimize the danger from all of these factors.

Like coal, oil can cause problems during extraction and transportation. Offshore oil drilling rigs can explode, harming workers and resulting in mass quantities of oil leaking from their wells. This occurred in 2010 with the *Deepwater Horizon* rig in the Gulf of Mexico, which the US federal government recognized as "the largest offshore oil spill in U.S. history."[18] Oil tankers, massive ships that transport enormous amounts of oil from port to port, can run aground or suffer damage, spilling their cargo into the sea. The most infamous example of this involved the tanker *Exxon Valdez*, which struck a reef off the coast of Alaska in 1989. Onshore oil pipelines can rupture and cause spills, too. Spilled oil can have catastrophic effects on the local wildlife and harm such industries as fishing and tourism.

All fossil fuels share a further weakness: their quantities are limited. The natural processes that create coal, oil, and natural gas take millions of years to happen. Over just a few centuries, humanity has significantly depleted Earth's supply of these resources. As the most accessible sources are used up, more time and money are needed to locate and extract deeper and harder-to-find fossil fuel sources. Increasing the cost to extract these fuels increases the cost of the resulting products. It is difficult to estimate exactly how many years' worth of coal, oil, and natural gas are left. The rates of using them can change, and new extraction technologies may make new deposits accessible. The controversial technology known as **fracking** has increased production in many areas. Still, scientists expect the production of fossil fuels to peak sometime in the next century. Researcher Richard Nehring found that "none of the fossil fuels, even with highly optimistic resource estimates, is projected to keep growing beyond 2050."[19] The supply situation for solar is dramatically different: the Sun's energy is essentially unlimited and is free to access.

While there may be decades' worth of fossil fuel supplies remaining, many experts are urging that they be left underground. The reason for this is perhaps the largest downside of using fossil fuels: climate change. The term *climate* describes the temperature, precipitation, and other atmospheric conditions over a long period of time. Throughout the course of Earth's history, the climate has gone through a variety of warming and cooling phases. But over the last several centuries, scientists have observed an unprecedented period of heating. During the same period, researchers have also measured a dramatic increase in the amount of carbon dioxide in the atmosphere. The vast majority of climate scientists are convinced that human activity, including the burning of fossil fuels, is responsible for the increasing carbon dioxide levels and temperatures. These two factors are connected by a phenomenon called the greenhouse effect.

When fossil fuels are burned, they release carbon dioxide and other gases. These emissions can be seen coming from power plant smokestacks and car tailpipes. The gases mix into the air around them and build up in the atmosphere. When sunlight comes through the atmosphere as visible light, it is able to pass through the greenhouse gases and reach the planet's surface. Some of this energy is reflected back upward as infrared light. The greenhouse gases allowed visible light to pass through them on the way down, but they absorb this reflected infrared light on the way up. This warms up the atmosphere. Some of this warmth is reflected back again toward the surface, further warming the planet.

The greenhouse effect occurs naturally. In fact, it is responsible for keeping Earth at a temperature comfortable for life. Without any greenhouse effect, the planet's surface temperature would be around 0°F (–18°C). However, greenhouse gases released by humans have accelerated the greenhouse effect. In 1958, scientists measured the concentration of carbon dioxide in the atmosphere at less than 320 parts per million (ppm). By 2015, the annual average carbon dioxide levels had risen to more than 400 ppm. As a result of the greenhouse effect, the US Environmental Protection Agency predicts "a likely increase of at least 2.7°F [1.5°C]" in the average global temperature by 2100.[20]

Rising temperatures can have a variety of negative effects. They may change rain and snowfall patterns, which can wreak havoc on established farming methods. The heat can lead to longer, more severe droughts and more intense heat waves. It can also provide the energy to fuel stronger, more destructive hurricanes. Warming also melts the planet's polar ice, leading to rising sea levels. Higher tides can threaten populous coastal areas around the globe.

Solar power provides a promising way to generate electricity without contributing to climate change. While they are operating, solar panels and solar thermal systems do not emit greenhouse gases. However, the manufacturing processes used to make solar power equipment releases greenhouse gases, mostly indirectly from using fossil fuel–generated electricity. The amount of carbon dioxide released by solar manufacturing depends on where the factory is located. China, for example, relies heavily upon coal-burning power plants. Researchers at Argonne National Laboratory and Northwestern University found "the carbon footprint of photovoltaic panels made in China is indeed about double that of those manufactured in Europe."[21] But this is offset over time as the system generates electricity from the Sun. As more solar power is used, factories that produce new panels may end up running on the Sun's power.

The spread of solar energy also has benefits in the economic and political arenas. Increased use of solar is helping to build a new, high-tech industry. Scientists and researchers are studying how to improve solar technology. Engineers and factory workers are developing ways to manufacture solar equipment more efficiently. Construction crews are needed to install solar panels, and technicians are needed to maintain them. As the solar industry grows, all this work will create thousands of new jobs. A move to solar will also allow the United States to shift away from purchasing fossil fuels from politically unstable regions, including countries in the Middle East. Instead, it will be able to rely more on a homegrown solar power industry.

Solar Challenges—Technical

Though solar power is a compelling energy source compared with fossil fuels, it is not without its own challenges and drawbacks. In determining whether solar power can replace fossil fuels, it is important to weigh all these factors. The most obvious problem with solar energy is that it does not work when the Sun isn't shining. At night, PV cells produce no energy, and in cloudy conditions their energy output is greatly reduced. Even on a clear day, the atmosphere prevents some of the Sun's energy from reaching cells on the surface.

Solar thermal plants can use heat-storing materials, such as molten salts, to continue producing electricity at night, but these make up only a small percentage of solar power systems. One solution for PV systems is to store electricity in batteries for use when the Sun isn't out, but this comes with its own challenges. Batteries are expensive to purchase, install, and maintain, and they increase the complexity of a power system.

Tying a solar power system into the existing electrical grid presents additional challenges. Some of these are technical hurdles, while others deal with the policies of utility companies and the government. Both types of concerns are shaping the future of home solar installations.

On the technical front, adding a large number of grid-tied solar power systems can put new stresses on the grid. When the Sun goes down, the electrical output of PV systems drops off. Evening is also the time when demand is often greatest, as people return home from work and use lights, appliances, and electronics. With solar output dropping, conventional power plants must quickly ramp up their generation to satisfy the demand. But these power plants typically take hours to start up and increase their output. One potential solution to this is to develop power plants that are more flexible, able to quickly raise or lower their output. Another fix is to ensure that grid-tied solar power systems include batteries to store the collected power. The batteries can continue sending electricity into the grid for a few hours after sunset, helping balance the load.

When a solar power system generates electricity, that power typically travels into an inverter and is converted from DC to AC before being used or sent into the grid. The inverter controls the voltage and frequency of the electricity it puts out. Technical troubles can arise when a wide variety of different inverters are putting electricity with various voltages and frequencies into the grid. This can make the grid unstable and unable to provide reliable power. Modern, standardized inverters can provide a steady flow of electricity.

Solar Challenges—Policy

Policy-wise, one major point of contention has been the concept of net metering. In this billing system, when utility customers with grid-tied home solar systems generate more power than they can

Net-Metering Solutions

Some local utilities are searching for solutions to the problems they find with net metering. In San Antonio, Texas, a utility introduced a program called SolarHost in 2015. Under this program, homeowners can apply to have a rooftop solar system installed on their house for free. The utility covers all the costs, buying the panels, installing them, and maintaining the system. Homeowners lease the space on their roofs to the utility, paying a discounted electricity rate in exchange.

The SolarHost program benefits both utilities and homeowners. For the utilities, it gives them a way to cover the fixed costs of distributing electricity, without relying on the varying income that net metering can cause. It also helps improve the grid's stability. Because the utility is buying and installing all the equipment, it can ensure that it is using standardized inverters and coordinating them to send a consistent output into the grid. For consumers, SolarHost broadens the availability of renewable energy to people who might not otherwise be able to afford a home solar installation. And since the utility covers maintenance costs, the homeowner doesn't need to worry about the time and money needed for upkeep.

use, the excess electricity goes back into the grid and the customer is paid for it. If a customer uses little electricity and generates a lot of it, his or her electric bill could even drop down to zero. Many solar customers argue that net metering is a fair way to compensate them for producing extra power for the grid.

However, utilities have argued that people who take advantage of these net-metering policies are not paying their fair share. Electric bills pay for more than just the power a customer receives. They also cover the costs of maintaining the grid, including installing new lines, trimming trees, and hiring emergency crews to respond to outages.

Though customers benefitting from net metering are still getting power from the utility at night, they are not contributing to these overhead costs. Utilities have convinced many state governments of the importance of this issue. More than thirty states have approved or are considering cuts to solar energy credits or the addition of new fees for grid-tied solar installations.

Solar Challenges—Environment

Though both photovoltaic and thermal solar power, unlike fossil fuels, are able to generate electricity without emitting greenhouse gases, they do introduce a few other environmental issues. In the case of PV panels, the process of manufacturing can release hazardous chemicals and be dangerous for workers. In the case of solar thermal power plants, the intense heat they generate can be dangerous to nearby wildlife.

Nearly all of today's solar cells are made from silicon. This material begins as quartz, which must be mined from underground. As with all kinds of mining, this carries risks for the miners. Refining quartz into silicon requires furnaces that generate very high temperatures. Running these furnaces takes a lot of energy, which today often comes from fossil fuel sources. Purifying silicon produces the toxic chemical silicon tetrachloride as a waste product. Manufacturers are supposed to recycle it. However, as *IEEE Spectrum* magazine reports, "the reprocessing equipment can cost tens of millions of dollars," so "some operations have just thrown away the by-product" to save money.[22] When silicon tetrachloride gets into the environment

Solar cells are commonly made from silicon. Manufacturing silicon can release pollutants into the environment.

and mixes with water, it forms hydrochloric acid, which can be dangerous to any plants, animals, and people nearby. Large numbers of people have been sickened in several such incidents in China, which has a huge solar industry but relatively loose environmental laws. However, recently adopted standards there have been stricter about recycling silicon tetrachloride.

Developing alternatives to silicon for use in solar cells may help reduce these risks and hazards. Thin-film cells avoid the use of silicon, though they often contain cadmium, a metal that has been linked to cancer. Companies must protect people who work with cadmium in the thin-film cell manufacturing process from exposure to it.

Thermal solar power plants also introduce new environmental concerns. Such issues have been on display at the Ivanpah CSP plant in California. The concentrated light at the plant, which heats up the air to high temperatures, can pose a severe threat to birds. When birds fly into these heated beams of light, they can catch fire and burn to death. Other birds die from colliding with the plant's three huge towers. In all, federal officials estimate that approximately six thousand birds per year die from these causes at Ivanpah. Gerry George, a renewable energy expert with an environmental organization in California, criticized the plant: "Ivanpah is a bird sink—and a cautionary tale unfolding on public lands."[23]

Ever since these problems were recognized, workers at Ivanpah have been trying to find solutions. They replaced the plant's original lighting system with LED bulbs. This lighting technology attracts fewer insects, which in turn attracts fewer of the birds that feed on those insects. On the towers, workers have added anti-perching spikes, installed machines that give off a substance that irritates birds, and put in place speakers that emit loud, high-pitched noises.

The Government Steps In

Government policies play an important role in whether solar power will be able to replace fossil fuels. For decades, the US government has given significant support to the fossil fuel industry. One report in 2015 found that "national subsidies to oil, gas and coal producers in the US amount to $20.5 billion annually."[24] The bulk of this assistance comes in the form of large tax breaks. For instance, when an oil company is involved in an oil spill that requires a big, expensive cleanup, it can count those costs as a regular business expense. This allows the company to pay less in taxes.

In recent years, the government has begun offering incentives for solar power installations. One of these, provided by state and local governments, involves tax exemptions. There are two types of these incentives: property tax exemptions and sales tax exemptions. In property tax exemptions, businesses or homeowners do not have to include the value of their solar power systems in the overall value of their property. This means they pay less money in property taxes. This type of incentive is offered by thirty-eight states. In sales tax exemptions, people do not need to pay sales taxes on solar power equipment and installations. Some form of sales tax exemption can be found in twenty-nine states.

Another federal government incentive program is known as the Solar Investment Tax Credit (ITC). The US Congress created the Solar ITC with the Energy Policy Act of 2005. The Solar ITC subtracts 30 percent of a solar system's cost from a homeowner's overall taxes. The Solar Industries Association declared, "The ITC is nothing short of a tax policy success story."[25] The success of the Solar ITC shows how continued support from the government can help solar technology become a strong competitor to fossil fuels.

HOW CAN VEHICLES
USE SOLAR ENERGY?

People use a huge amount of energy powering vehicles, and nearly all of that energy comes from fossil fuels. In the United States, transportation made up about 29 percent of all energy use in 2016. Of that, about 95 percent came from oil or natural gas. Electricity provided less than 1 percent of the energy used for transportation.

Researchers and engineers are seeking ways to expand the use of electricity in vehicles. When that electricity is produced using renewable technologies, this results in dramatic reductions in greenhouse gas emissions. Sometimes this electricity comes from the grid and is produced by hydroelectric dams, wind farms, or solar power plants. But in some cases, solar panels allow a vehicle to produce its own power without relying on the grid.

The promise of solar-powered vehicles that can drive, fly, or motor through the oceans without needing to be refueled is compelling.

However, there are several challenges that these vehicles face. First, the low efficiency of PV panels means that relatively little power can be produced, even with solar cells covering the vehicle's entire surface. Solar-powered vehicles usually must be extremely lightweight and delicate to work, limiting their usefulness in carrying passengers and cargo. Another challenge is that the Sun does not always shine. Such vehicles must carry batteries, which often add significant weight, to continue operating at night or in cloudy weather.

The challenges are daunting, but engineers have not been deterred. In recent years, they have made major breakthroughs in solar-powered vehicles. A spacecraft exploring Jupiter used solar power farther away from the Sun than any spacecraft had before. Solar panels help charge batteries on some electric cars. An airplane and a boat each completed journeys around the globe powered entirely by solar cells. Continued efforts in this field are pushing the boundaries of solar technology forward, and they may end up changing the world of transportation forever.

Solar in Space

The first solar cells to fly into space launched in March 1958 on the *Vanguard 1* spacecraft. This tiny probe, only about the size of a large grapefruit, was the second satellite ever launched from the United States. It carried six small silicon-based solar cells, together generating about 1 watt of electricity at an efficiency of around 10 percent. Since the time of *Vanguard 1*, solar cells have become a critical part of many different spacecraft. Some spacecraft use

This illustration shows the Dawn spacecraft in orbit. The Dawn spacecraft is equipped with solar panels that generate electricity, which powers the spacecraft's ion thrusters.

the electricity generated by solar cells to propel themselves through space. Others simply use the electrical power to operate their computers and scientific instruments, relying on traditional rocket engines to push themselves through space.

Launched in September 2007 on a mission to explore the asteroids Vesta and Ceres, the *Dawn* spacecraft is an example of the former category. Its two solar arrays, each measuring 7.6 feet (2.3 m) by 27.2 feet (8.3 m), generate electricity to power the spacecraft's ion thrusters. In this type of engine, electricity is used to **ionize** xenon gas and accelerate it out the back of the spacecraft, pushing the spacecraft forward. Ion thrusters produce much weaker thrust than traditional rocket engines, but they are vastly more efficient. Because they use xenon gas so slowly, they can be fired for weeks at a time, allowing the spacecraft to gradually pick up speed. All the while, *Dawn's* huge solar arrays provide a constant source of electricity. Thanks to the low acceleration, spacecraft propelled by ion engines often have long-duration missions. *Dawn* reached Vesta in July 2011, and it finally got to Ceres in March 2015.

The *Juno* spacecraft, launched in August 2011, broke new ground for solar-powered space flight. The spacecraft's mission, according to NASA, is to help scientists "understand the origin and evolution of Jupiter."[26] *Juno* used a traditional rocket engine to reach Jupiter, but during its mission it generated electricity using PV solar cells. This made it the most distant mission to use the Sun as its power source. One of the challenges with using solar cells in space is that the energy of sunlight diminishes rapidly when traveling away from the Sun. At Earth's distance from the Sun, a 10.8-square-foot (1.0-sq-m) solar array produces about 400 watts of electricity. At Jupiter's distance (484 million miles [779 million km]), that array would need to measure about 269 square feet (25 sq m) to produce the same amount of power. And at Pluto's distance (3.67 billion miles [5.91 billion km]), it would need to be about 21,500 square feet (2,000 sq m)—larger than four basketball courts.

Solar Power on the ISS

Solar arrays in space are also useful closer to home, on the International Space Station (ISS). The ISS orbits Earth at an altitude of about 250 miles (400 km). Its first piece launched in 1998. Over the next few decades, a group of fifteen countries worked together to add new parts and modules at a total cost of about $100 billion. The volume of the station that is fit for human life is now greater than that of a five-bedroom house. Since November 2, 2000, there has been a constant human presence on the station. Today there is typically a crew of six people at any given time. Crew members rotate on and off the station every few months.

To support the people and equipment of the ISS requires a lot of electricity. The station has eight solar arrays, each measuring 112 feet (34 m) by 39 feet (12 m). Astronauts installed them over the course of several missions during the station's construction phase. The huge arrays could not launch at their full, extended size. Instead, they were folded up for launch. Once they were in space, they were expanded to their enormous spans. They are designed so that they tilt to follow the Sun. Together, the arrays can generate up to 120 kilowatts of electricity. The ISS is also equipped with a battery system so that it can power itself when it passes over the night side of Earth and the planet blocks the Sun's rays.

Typically, spacecraft use photovoltaics only in the inner solar system, where the sunlight is relatively bright. The inner solar system includes Mercury, Venus, Earth, and Mars. But *Juno* used the panels all the way out near Jupiter, located in the outer solar system, when it reached the planet in July 2016. To get enough power at that distance, *Juno*'s engineers equipped the spacecraft with three enormous solar panels containing a total of almost 19,000 cells. When the spacecraft was near Earth, the solar cells would be capable of producing about 14,000 watts. At Jupiter, they would generate around 400 watts. The spacecraft's team made sure to use computers and equipment that could operate on little power, and the mission planners designed a **trajectory** that would take *Juno* around Jupiter's poles, avoiding passing behind the planet into shadow. Scott Bolton, one of the project's lead scientists, noted that despite these challenges, solar power seemed a fitting option for *Juno*:

We use every known technique to see through Jupiter's clouds and reveal the secrets Jupiter holds of our solar system's early history. It just seems right that the Sun is helping us learn about the origin of Jupiter and the other planets that orbit it.[27]

Solar Cars

Solar power is an ideal source of energy in space. When using it for propulsion, the spacecraft does not face air resistance, and when using it for electrical power, there is no atmosphere to diminish or block the Sun's rays, as well as no nighttime or weather to interfere. On Earth's surface, using solar power in vehicles is much more challenging. Still, many engineers are rising to the challenge of using photovoltaic cells to power cars.

October 22, 2015, was a bright, sunny day in Adelaide, Australia. Under a brilliant blue sky, a wide, low vehicle with a curved top zoomed along the city's roads. Covering the car were sheets of solar cells. On the right side of the vehicle, a glassy bump rose above the panels. The driver's head was visible in this bubble. The solar car rolled across a finish line, cheered on by gathered crowds of people. The vehicle, known as Nuna 8, was built by a team from Delft University of Technology in the Netherlands. It had just won the 2015 World Solar Challenge. The team's manager, Mark Hupkens, said, "We were on the edge of what our machine is able to do and we made it."[28]

The World Solar Challenge is a solar car race that takes drivers on a journey of more than 1,850 miles (3,000 km) across Australia, from Darwin in the far north to Adelaide in the far south. The race began in 1987. Since 1999, the race has been held every two years. According to the World Solar Challenge's website, the purpose of the competition is "to develop the most efficient electric vehicles possible."[29] The vehicles involved are far from practical for everyday use. Nuna 8, for example, weighs just 330 pounds (150 kg), carries a single person, and lacks the safety standards required in modern cars. Its 391 silicon solar cells generate approximately 1 kilowatt of electricity at an efficiency of about 24 percent. This is about one-sixtieth the energy that can be generated by a car burning fossil fuels in an **internal combustion engine**.

While it is unlikely that anything like the Nuna 8 will be taking over the world's roads, some more traditional cars have begun to incorporate solar panels into their design. The 2010 model of the Toyota Prius, a popular hybrid car that incorporates both an internal combustion engine and an electric motor, featured a small panel on its roof. However, the panel did not charge the large batteries used for driving. Instead, it only powered a ventilation fan that helped keep the car cool while it was parked. In 2017, Toyota added an option for a larger panel that could be used to extend the Prius's range. Due to the small surface area of the roof, the low efficiency of solar panels, and the high power demands of driving, the benefit was relatively minor. A sunny day's worth of electricity adds approximately 2.2 miles (3.5 km) to the vehicle's range. The system faced legal limitations, too. Because the panel is covered in glass sheeting that doesn't comply with US auto safety regulations, the solar Prius was available only in Europe and Japan. However, despite these challenges, the car's makers saw a bright future for a mainstream car with solar power. Prius engineer Koji Toyoshima said, "It should be possible to do a lot of charging this way in places like California or Arizona."[30]

Flying on Sunlight

For decades, engineers have worked to develop solar-powered aircraft. Solar power is uniquely suited to aircraft in several ways. First, an aircraft can have broad, light wings, providing a great deal of surface area for solar panels. Many aircraft fly high enough to soar above most clouds, providing unblocked access to sunlight during the day. However, there are also important drawbacks. As with cars, traditional fossil fuel–powered engines provide airplanes with huge amounts of power. Even large wings covered in solar panels can generate only a fraction of the energy needed by traditional aircraft. This means that solar airplanes must be extremely light. This results

NASA's Helios Prototype was tested in a flight over the Pacific Ocean in 2001. This remotely controlled aircraft had a sustained flight time of 40 minutes during its test run.

in designs that are dramatically different from standard aircraft and which can carry very little weight in cargo and passengers. Additionally, solar aircraft face the same challenge that all uses of solar power must contend with: night. To fly one of these planes at night, the panels must charge onboard batteries during the day and then run off this stored electricity after sunset. The heavy batteries further complicate the design process.

One of the first major successes in the field of solar aircraft was the Helios Prototype, developed in the late 1990s and early 2000s by NASA and the aerospace corporation AeroVironment. Measuring 247 feet (75 m) from wingtip to wingtip, its wingspan is broader than that of a military cargo plane or a commercial airliner. This enormous wing, measuring 8 feet (2.4 m) from front to back, is completely covered in solar cells. Some 62,000 silicon-based cells operate at an efficiency of about 19 percent, generating electricity to power the aircraft.

According to NASA, the purpose of the Helios design is "to carry a payload of scientific instruments or telecommunications relay equipment averaging about 200 lb [91 kg] to high altitudes for missions."[31] The Helios is controlled remotely from the ground. The wing makes up essentially the entire aircraft—there is no traditional body or tail. The whole vehicle weighs approximately 2,000 pounds (900 kg), less than one-fifth of the weight of a single engine from a modern airliner. A series of fourteen motors with propellers, mounted across the back of the wing, push Helios forward. It cruises at a speed of up to 27 miles per hour (43 kmh), dramatically slower than traditional aircraft. Helios may be slow, but it has impressive altitude capabilities. On a record-setting flight on August 13, 2001, it ascended to an altitude of 96,863 feet (29,524 m). In comparison, passenger jets typically fly at altitudes of less than 40,000 feet (12,000 m).

A solar-powered airplane made history again in July 2016. In that month, Solar Impulse 2 completed the first around-the-world flight by a plane powered by solar cells. The plane had left Abu Dhabi, United Arab Emirates, in March 2015. More than a year later, following multiple flights and weeks-long stops, it touched down in the same city. Ban Ki-moon, then secretary-general to the United

Nations, announced: "The journey to a more sustainable world is just beginning. The Solar Impulse team is helping to pilot us to that future."[32]

Solar Impulse 2 looks much more like a traditional plane than Helios. It has a cockpit for a single pilot, a tail, and a broad wing. Similar to Helios, this wing is covered in solar cells—more than 17,000 of them. Because the aircraft is designed to fly at night as well as in the day, it contains batteries. These batteries make up about one-quarter of *Solar Impulse 2*'s overall weight of 5,070 pounds (2,300 kg). In the day, it flies at an altitude up to 29,000 feet (8,800 m) and its solar cells feed extra electricity into the batteries. At night it slows down, drops to 5,000 feet (1,500 m), and uses that stored energy until sunrise.

The Swiss pilots Bertrand Piccard and André Borschberg shared flying duties on the *Solar Impulse 2*'s round-the-world mission, alternating at each stop. The longest part of the journey was the five-day flight from Japan to Hawaii, covering 4,000 miles (6,400 km). Conditions inside *Solar Impulse 2* were rough. There was no heating system, and the pilot's seat doubled as a toilet during the long flight. The mission encountered long delays caused by windy conditions and overheating batteries. The pilots and engineers persisted, and they completed the historic journey.

After the flight, Piccard described how he hoped that *Solar Impulse 2* would inspire people: "All the clean technologies we use, they can be used everywhere. So we have flown 40,000 km [25,000 mi], but now it is up to other people to take it further."[33]

Solar at Sea

In June 2016, engineer Damon McMillan waded out into the surf of Half Moon Bay, California. He carried an 8-foot- (2.4-m-) long flat-topped boat. Solar panels covered its upper surface, providing electricity for a small propeller and steering system below the water. Onboard computer systems and satellite communications equipment, sealed away from corrosive seawater, allowed McMillan to monitor its location and send it commands remotely. The engineer and his small team of hobbyists called the vessel *SeaCharger*. They had built it over the course of two and a half years. McMillan released it into the water, and it began moving west. Then he flew to Hawaii.

Forty-one days later, McMillan waited in Hawaii's Mahukona Harbor. He spotted *SeaCharger* on the horizon. Using a remote control, he steered it into the harbor, and his wife swam out to grab the boat. The foam-and-fiberglass *SeaCharger* had completed a journey of 2,400 miles (3,860 km) entirely on solar power. McMillan reported: "I know that this is the same SeaCharger that left California . . . but the faded paint and clinging barnacles only hint at what it must have experienced—and survived—to get here."[34]

Though it is small, *SeaCharger* demonstrates the potential of using solar power for ocean travel. Land vehicles must overcome friction with the road, and airplanes must keep up their speed to stay in the air. But boats can float upon the water and move along at a relatively leisurely pace if they need to. *SeaCharger* crossed the Pacific Ocean at just 2.9 miles per hour (4.7 kmh). By comparison, modern cargo ships move at around 23–29 miles per hour (37–47 kmh).

Small-scale projects like *SeaCharger* demonstrate that powering boats with photovoltaics is within the reach of ordinary people. However, there has also been progress in much larger solar vessels. In May 2012, following a journey that began in September 2010, the MS *Tûranor PlanetSolar* became the first solar-powered ship to circle the globe. Measuring 115 feet (35 m) long and weighing in at 196,000 pounds (88,900 kg), the vessel dwarfs the *SeaCharger.* It has six rooms inside and can support nine crew members. The entire upper deck of the *PlanetSolar,* an area of 5,500 square feet (511 sq m), is covered in solar cells. Inside the hull, 8.5 short tons (7.7 metric t) of batteries store energy so that the ship can keep moving at night or on cloudy days.

Engineers designed the *PlanetSolar* to maximize the energy it gets from the Sun and minimize the energy it takes to move. The sturdy solar panels, which can support the weight of a crew member walking on them, have an efficiency of 19 percent. The angles on some of them can be adjusted to get more direct sunlight, and layers of plastic protect the panels from seawater. Computer systems on the ship's bridge show predictions of cloud cover on the seas ahead. This lets the crew plot a course that keeps them in sunlight wherever possible. Finally, the boat's double-hull design allows it to move through the water more smoothly than a single-hull design would. It results in less

PlanetSolar *is the world's largest solar-powered vessel. Its upper deck is covered in solar panels.*

drag, meaning the engines do not have to work as hard and use as much electricity. The *PlanetSolar* can move at a maximum speed of 16 miles per hour (26 kmh).

The *PlanetSolar* was developed by Swiss engineer Raphaël Domjan and French sailor Gérard D'Aboville. Their high-tech, solar-powered vessel demonstrated that photovoltaics can be useful in boats at a large scale. After its world-circling journey, the ship was used for scientific missions. Because it doesn't use fossil-fuel engines that emit exhaust gases, it can carry out sensitive measurements of ocean currents and particles in the atmosphere without worrying about contamination.

Domjan noted that the overall reason for building *PlanetSolar* was "to spread optimism, because almost everybody on this planet knows we have to change, but they think we cannot change."[35]

WHAT IS THE FUTURE OF SOLAR POWER?

With prices falling and technology improving, solar power has come a long way in recent years. However, it remains a relatively tiny part of overall world energy production. Scientists and engineers are studying how to change this. Some are researching how to improve today's solar cell designs using innovative materials and techniques. Others are finding ways to put solar cells into new places by making them blend in with modern architecture. On the most basic level, poor countries, with millions of people lacking electricity, represent an opportunity for solar power to dramatically change lives for the better. On the advanced end of the spectrum, some of the cutting-edge technologies on the drawing board include artificial leaves, solar paint, and even satellites that beam solar power back to Earth. All of these areas of development may play a role in the future of solar power.

New Materials

Presently, silicon is by far the most popular material for making commercial solar cells. The industry is very familiar with manufacturing these cells, silicon is relatively plentiful, and the cells can generate electricity with moderate efficiency. However, researchers are exploring new materials, such as perovskite, that could potentially replace silicon. Perovskite is a manufactured material that has the same crystal structure as the mineral calcium titanium oxide, also called perovskite. Perovskite materials are usually made when organic molecules such as carbon and hydrogen bind with metal, such as lead, and elements called halogens, such as chlorine.

Early research on perovskite materials in solar cells began around 2009. In these initial tests, the efficiency of the resulting cells was less than 5 percent, much lower than the efficiency of silicon cells. However, significant improvements followed, and scientists have reached efficiencies of more than 20 percent in the laboratory. The potential efficiency, then, is similar to silicon cells. But perovskite offers many potential advantages. It is much cheaper than silicon. And while silicon cells require difficult, precise processes to make, the manufacturing of perovskite cells would be simpler.

Perovskite may also be a good complement to silicon. By layering both materials in a single solar cell, more energy could be captured. The bandgap of perovskite is about 1.4 eV, compared with silicon's 1.1 eV, meaning less energy is lost and more electricity can be generated. Researcher Michael McGehee of Stanford University believes this is an especially interesting area of research, saying, "I think this is one of the more compelling [pathways] because it's not going head to head with silicon, it's partnering with silicon."[36]

These benefits are promising, but perovskite still faces several challenges as a material for solar cells. Though an efficiency level high enough to be useful has been reached in the lab, these results have not been replicated when tested in real-world conditions. These lab-tested cells are also very small, measuring less than 0.16 square inches (1 sq cm) in area. Making the cells at larger sizes has been difficult. Finally, these cells have not proven to be as durable as their silicon counterparts. Nitin Padture, a professor of materials science at Brown University, has found that "when you expose these cells to humid air, they basically degrade in a couple of days or weeks."[37] In the same conditions, silicon cells can remain productive for several years. Clearing all these hurdles will take time. In 2016, researchers estimated that the commercial use of perovskite solar cells could still be a decade away.

Blending In

In the fall of 2016, entrepreneur Elon Musk made a major solar power announcement. Musk has a history of disrupting high-tech industries. His company SpaceX made pioneering advances in reusable rockets, pushing down the cost of satellite launches. His company Tesla developed stylish, popular electric cars that proved consumers were interested in moving away from fossil fuels. Now, Musk announced that Tesla and its partner, the company SolarCity, were ready to advance the solar power industry with a new product: solar roofs.

Ordinarily, installing a home solar power system means placing large, heavy panels on a roof, along with brackets and other mounting hardware. The appearance of all these materials is off-putting to some customers. Even if customers are interested in solar power, they may not like the look of this bulky equipment on their roof. Traditional panels, unlike Musk's solar roofs, also require regular maintenance. Musk's solar roofs are aimed at people who want more user-friendly solar power systems that will blend in with their home. His companies' solution is to put the solar cells inside the roofing tiles themselves. Coatings on the tiles make them look like ordinary roofing materials from a distance. But whenever the Sun is shining, they are generating clean power for a customer's home.

The solar roof may help make solar power more popular, but it still faces some challenges. Though the coatings help the roofing tiles look nicer, they also block a small amount of sunlight, reducing efficiency. The temperature of the solar roof could be an issue, too. Standard solar panels are mounted so that there is a gap between them and the roof. This allows airflow to help cool them, since overheating can reduce the efficiency of solar cells. The solar roofing tiles would not permit this kind of cooling. Finally, the solar roof will need to work well as a roof. Standard roofs are sturdy enough to protect against harsh weather, such as hail. If the solar roofing tiles are not at least as strong, their usefulness may be limited. Responding to this concern,

Musk showed a video demonstration at his 2016 presentation. In the video, a weight is dropped on several common roofing materials, as well as on one of the solar roof tiles. Tiles made of terra cotta, clay, and slate shattered under the blow. The solar tile remained intact. If the solar roofing system can live up to its promise, it may help change the way people think about installing solar on their own homes.

At the end of his presentation, Musk said that he expected people to be proud to show off their solar roofs:

> I think the key is really to make solar something desirable where if you install a solar roof in your house, you're really proud. You want to put it on the most prominent part of the house.[38]

The Developing World

While people in the developed world can often afford large home solar panels, the situation is much different in **developing countries**. In 2009, more than 1.3 billion people in the world did not have access to electricity at all. For many of these people, lighting still comes in the form of candles or **kerosene** lamps. There is a major opportunity for small-scale solar power to improve lives using solar lanterns.

Solar lanterns are simple devices that have 2- to 5-watt solar cells, low-power light-emitting **diodes** (LEDs), and a small battery for storing electricity at night or on cloudy days. They provide more light than a kerosene lantern, and experts estimate that nearly everyone who uses a kerosene lantern would be able to afford one of these lanterns. The cost is offset by the fact that the consumer would no longer need to buy kerosene. Instead, the consumer would get free, clean energy from the Sun. Some of these lanterns even include ports for charging devices, such as cell phones. This can help people in poor, rural areas stay connected with family and friends. Solar lanterns have already proven popular, with more than 5 million sold worldwide by 2015. However, with so many people still lacking reliable access to electricity, there is much more room for growth.

In a study on the potential of solar power in developing nations, MIT concluded:

> [U]nique opportunities are beginning to emerge as a result of low solar prices for small grid systems powered exclusively with solar PV that can provide primary and backup power in rural areas where the realization of reliable grid power is decades in the future.[39]

By moving straight to solar power and skipping the traditional grid system that has long been present in developed nations, the

Kenyan fishermen use a floating solar lantern to fish at night in Lake Victoria. Solar lanterns, which include chargeable batteries, are one of the few solar technologies available to people in the developing world.

developing world has the opportunity to build clean, sustainable infrastructure from the ground up.

New Technologies

The future of solar energy may take inspiration from the natural world. In a way, plants use solar power every day in the process of photosynthesis, creating food for themselves with the inputs of carbon dioxide, water, and sunlight. The new field of artificial photosynthesis aims to recreate this process, using it to create a liquid fuel rather than food for plants.

Researchers Daniel Nocera and Pamela Silver of Harvard University are working in this area. In the process they have developed, an artificial leaf is dropped into water. The artificial leaf is a silicon solar cell with the added **catalysts** cobalt phosphate and a metal compound made up of nickel and zinc. When sunlight hits the leaf, these catalysts split the water into oxygen and hydrogen.

The hydrogen, along with carbon dioxide from the atmosphere, can then be fed to bacteria that have been specifically engineered to convert these gases into a liquid fuel. Nocera describes the artificial leaf as "a true artificial photosynthesis system."[40] In nature, photosynthesis has an efficiency of about 1 percent. In other words, 1 percent of the solar energy that hits the plant ends up becoming energy in the plant's food. The artificial leaf is capable of 10 percent efficiency. This technology could someday provide a way for people to create their own vehicle fuel at home rather than having to drive to a gas station.

Other researchers are investigating the potential of road surfaces to act as solar panels. Idaho-based technology company Solar Roadways is developing hexagonal solar panels covered in durable glass. Engineers at Solar Roadways are experimenting with different types of solar cells, including thin-film and traditional silicon PV cells, to determine which will be most efficient. The panels are designed with internal heating systems so that the solar cells do not freeze in cold temperatures, which would provide the added benefit of melting ice and snow on roadways. According to the company's website, LED lights inside the glass would "warn drivers of impending danger" and make "road lines more visible."[41] In addition, the panels under development by Solar Roadways might be able to charge electric vehicles. Charging plates in the panels create an electromagnetic field, and when an electric-powered vehicle drives over these charging plates, this charges the vehicle's battery.

Another technology now under development is solar paint. Rather than having to install rigid solar panels, a person could simply coat any surface in solar paint to collect the energy from sunlight. Many scientists are working with materials known as quantum dots. These tiny crystals of semiconductors are mixed into a liquid and are then painted onto a surface. Susanna Thon, assistant professor of electrical and computer engineering at Johns Hopkins University, says, "Unlike silicon—which has a set absorption profile—with quantum dots, by just changing their diameter, you can change the portion of the spectrum they absorb."[42] When sunlight hits the solar paint, the semiconductors generate electricity.

The downside is that present solar paint technology has a low efficiency, ranging from 3 to 11 percent among the types of solar paint now being studied. Much more research and development will be needed to improve the efficiencies of solar paint. But if more progress can be made, solar paint may make up an important part of the solar energy industry of tomorrow.

Space-Based Solar Power

The Sun gives off an incredible amount of energy. If people could capture all of the sunlight that hits Earth in a single hour, that energy would power the planet for a whole year. But much of that energy never reaches Earth's surface. None can be captured at night, and during the day, clouds and the atmosphere itself block some of it. Of the light that hits the top of the atmosphere, only about 30 percent reaches the planet's surface. One proposed solution to this problem is known as space-based solar power.

Space-based solar power would involve launching huge satellites into space, where they would collect unfiltered light from the Sun. Then they would beam the power back to Earth. Ground stations would receive this energy, turn it into electricity, and send it into the electrical grid. Some governments are investigating the possibilities of space-based solar power. There are two basic types of this system being studied. One uses **microwaves** to beam energy back to Earth, and the other uses **lasers**.

Microwave-transmitting satellites would orbit high above the planet, circling Earth at an altitude of about 21,700 miles (34,900 km). This would put them in a geostationary orbit. This means they would travel around the planet at

> ## WORDS IN CONTEXT
>
> **microwaves**
> Electromagnetic waves with wavelengths ranging from 0.003 to 0.98 feet (0.001–0.3 m).
>
> **lasers**
> Devices that generate intense, focused beams of light.

the same speed the planet is rotating below them. The result is that they would remain above a fixed point on Earth's surface. However, this distant orbit would also make it difficult to reach the satellite if repairs are needed.

The satellites in this type of solar power system would be huge, stretching approximately 2 miles (3 km) wide and weighing more than 170 million pounds (80 million kg). This is far too large to launch with a single rocket. Instead, a satellite would have to be launched in dozens of pieces and then assembled in space. The total cost could reach tens of billions of dollars.

Back on the ground, the receiving station would need to be several miles wide, since the microwave beam would spread out considerably over the long distance. Despite all of these challenges and expenses, a microwave-transmitting satellite "would be capable of generating multiple gigawatts of power, enough to power a major U.S. city," according to the US Department of Energy.[43]

A system using laser-transmitting satellites would look significantly different. The satellites would orbit at a relatively close 250 miles (400 km), about as far away as the ISS. Each would weigh less than 22,000 pounds (10,000 kg), meaning a satellite could be sent up in a single rocket. Experts estimate the cost of building, launching, and operating one of these satellites at about $500 million.

Tightly focused laser beams are much narrower than microwave beams, so the ground station could be relatively small. In order to

Major Players in Solar Power

Many countries are positioning themselves to be future leaders in the solar industry. Pollution caused by fossil-fuel power plants became a severe issue in China, but the country has sought cleaner energy sources in the last decade. By 2015, it produced almost two-thirds of the world's solar panels. Its increased production has helped drive down solar prices. In Japan, a 2011 accident at the Fukushima nuclear power plant made leaders interested in developing alternative power sources, including solar power. Among its efforts is increased research in space-based solar power. Elsewhere in Asia, India pledged in 2014 to develop twenty-five solar power plants generating 500 megawatts each. Even Saudi Arabia, best known for its leadership in oil production, plans to develop both photovoltaics and thermal solar power to take advantage of its hot and sunny climate.

Solar power continues to grow in the United States, too. In 2016, companies installed a record 14.6 gigawatts of new solar panels—nearly double the figure from the previous year. The solar industry accounted for 2 percent of all new jobs in the country that year. In the United States and across the world, it appears that solar power has become firmly established.

receive and transmit power from these laser beams, the ground station would need to be just a few meters across. However, the power generated would be only 1 to 10 megawatts per satellite. A large group of these satellites may have to be sent up together to generate the kind of power needed by cities.

Though neither microwave-transmitting nor laser-transmitting systems have been sent into space yet, some early work has been done on the ground. In 2008, an experiment in Hawaii received 20 watts worth of microwaves sent from 93 miles (150 km) away. And in 2014, a test in Japan demonstrated the transmission of

10 kilowatts of microwaves at a distance of 1,600 feet (500 m). Japan has long been a leader in the study of space-based solar power systems. Its official goal is to create a 1-gigawatt microwave system by the 2030s. According to Ralph Nansen, researcher for the US advocacy organization Solar High Study Group, "I don't think there's any doubt that within the next century we will be getting the majority of our power from space. It's just a question of when."[44]

A Solar-Powered Future

Solar power has come a long way since ancient times, when people oriented their houses to take advantage of the Sun's heating. In the 1950s, scientists learned how to turn the Sun's light into electricity. In the last several decades, major advances have been made in both solar thermal technologies and photovoltaics technologies. On the thermal side, rooftop collectors heat water for homes, and enormous CSP stations focus sunlight to create temperatures that can then be used to generate hundreds of megawatts of electricity. On the photovoltaics side, sunlight makes electricity for wristwatches, households, and vast arrays of solar panels.

Solar power provides significant benefits over the fossil fuels that have powered the world for more than a century. It is a clean, free, virtually unlimited source of energy, and it represents a key way in which people can begin to slow the effects of climate change. As technology improves and prices fall, solar continues to become an ever more attractive alternative to fossil fuels. Experimental uses in vehicles in space, in the air, on land, and at sea have demonstrated

Many cities, such as Shanghai in China, continue to develop solar power. Solar power's advantages over fossil fuels make it an attractive renewable energy source.

the potential of solar power to eventually replace traditional energy sources for some kinds of transport.

In 2015, MIT produced a study called *The Future of Solar Energy*. In it, a group of professors and distinguished experts from a variety of fields concluded, "Solar energy has recently become a rapidly growing source of electricity worldwide. . . . As a result the solar industry has become global in important respects."[45]

Technologies developed by scientists and engineers, as well as the policies developed by government officials, will determine the applications and advancements of solar power over the next several decades. Advances in both areas could lead to a bright future for solar energy and for humanity as a whole.

INTRODUCTION: POWERED BY SUNLIGHT

1. "California Clean Energy Tour Solar Star Projects," *California Energy Commission*, n.d. www.energy.ca.gov.

2. Quoted in Eric Wesoff, "Solar Star, Largest PV Power Plant in the World, Now Operational," *Greentech Media*, June 26, 2015. www.greentechmedia.com.

3. "The Future of Solar Energy," *Massachusetts Institute of Technology*, 2015. www.energy.mit.edu.

4. "New Energy Outlook 2017," *Bloomberg New Energy Finance*, 2017. www.about.bnef.com.

5. Quoted in John Fialka, "Are We Entering the Photovoltaic Energy Era?" *Scientific American*, December 15, 2016. www.scientificamerican.com.

CHAPTER 1: HOW DOES SOLAR POWER WORK?

6. Quoted in Lee Phillips, "The Future of Solar Energy Is Bright," *Ars Technica*, February 16, 2017. www.arstechnica.com.

7. "Solar Water Heaters," *US Department of Energy*, n.d. www.energy.gov.

8. Quoted in "World's Tallest Tower Goes Solar, Saving 3,200 kwh/Day," *Go Green*, n.d. www.go-green.ae.

9. "Ivanpah," *BrightSource Limitless*, n.d. www.brightsourceenergy.com.

10. Quoted in "April 25, 1954: Bell Labs Demonstrates the First Practical Silicon Solar Cell," *American Physical Society*, n.d. www.aps.org.

11. "Seven Surprising Realities behind the Great Transition to Renewable Energy," *Earth Policy Institute*, May 13, 2015. www.earth-policy.org.

12. "Solar Performance and Efficiency," *US Department of Energy*, August 20, 2013. www.energy.gov.

13. Karl W. Böer, "Solar Heating and Cooling of Buildings—Results and Implications of the Delaware Experiment," *National Science Foundation*, November 18–20, 1973. www.babel.hathitrust.org.

14. "Harnessing Solar Energy at Home," *US Department of Energy*, October 1, 2014. www.energy.gov.

15. Quoted in David Reid, "Kamuthi: The World's Largest Solar Power Project," *BBC*, May 24, 2017. www.bbc.com.

CHAPTER 2: CAN SOLAR POWER REPLACE FOSSIL FUELS?

16. "What Is U.S. Electricity Generation by Energy Source?" *US Energy Information Administration*, n.d. www.eia.gov.

17. "Mining: A Hazardous Work," *International Labour Organization*, 2017. www.ilo.org.

18. "*Deepwater Horizon* Oil Spill: Final Programmatic Damage Assessment and Restoration Plan and Final Programmatic Environmental Impact Statement," *National Oceanic and Atmospheric Administration*, February 2016. www.gulfspillrestoration.noaa.gov.

19. Richard Nehring, "Traversing the Mountaintop: World Fossil Fuel Production to 2050," *National Center for Biotechnology Information*, October 27, 2009. www.ncbi.nlm.nih.gov.

20. "Future of Climate Change," *United States Environmental Protection Agency*, December 27, 2016. www.epa.gov.

21. Quoted in Dustin Mulvaney, "Solar Energy Isn't Always as Green as You Think," *IEEE Spectrum*, November 13, 2014. www.spectrum.ieee.org.

22. Quoted in Mulvaney, "Solar Energy Isn't Always as Green as You Think."

23. Quoted in Louis Sahagun, "This Mojave Desert Solar Plant Kills 6,000 Birds a Year. Here's Why That Won't Change Any Time Soon," *Los Angeles Times*, September 2, 2016. www.latimes.com.

24. Quoted in Avaneesh Pandey, "US Fossil Fuel Subsidies Increase 'Dramatically' Despite Climate Change Pledge," *International Business Times*, November 12, 2015. www.ibtimes.com.

25. "Solar Investment Tax Credit (ITC)," *Solar Energy Industries Association*, 2017. www.seia.org.

CHAPTER 3: HOW CAN VEHICLES USE SOLAR ENERGY?

26. "Juno Overview," *National Aeronautics and Space Administration*, August 3, 2017. www.nasa.gov.

27. Quoted in "NASA's Juno Spacecraft Breaks Solar Power Distance Record," *NASA Jet Propulsion Laboratory*, January 13, 2016. www.jpl.nasa.gov.

28. Quoted in Michael Coggan, "Dutch Team Nuon Celebrate Victory in World Solar Challenge Race from Darwin to Adelaide," *ABC News*, October 22, 2015. www.abc.net.au.

29. "History," *Bridgestone World Solar Challenge*, n.d. www.worldsolarchallenge.org.

30. Quoted in Ronan Glon, "Why You Can't Order a Toyota Prius with a Roof-Mounted Solar Panel," *Digital Trends*, June 17, 2016. www.digitaltrends.com.

31. "NASA Armstrong Fact Sheet: Helios Prototype," *National Aeronautics and Space Administration*, February 28, 2014. www.nasa.gov.

32. Quoted in Damian Carrington, "Solar Plane Makes History after Completing Round-the-World Trip," *Guardian*, July 25, 2016. www.theguardian.com.

33. Quoted in Carrington, "Solar Plane Makes History after Completing Round-the-World Trip."

34. Quoted in Damon McMillan, "Did a Solar-Powered Autonomous Boat Just Cross the Pacific Ocean?" *Maker Media*, August 22, 2016. www.makezine.com.

35. Quoted in Christopher Mims, "World's Mightiest Solar Boat Unveiled," *Scientific American*, March 1, 2010. www.scientificamerican.com.

CHAPTER 4: WHAT IS THE FUTURE OF SOLAR POWER?

36. Quoted in Chelsea Harvey, "This Technology May Be the Future of Solar Energy," *Washington Post*, January 15, 2016. www.washingtonpost.com.

37. Quoted in Harvey, "This Technology May Be the Future of Solar Energy."

38. Quoted in "Tesla Unveils Powerwall 2 and Solar Roof," *YouTube*, October 28, 2016. www.youtube.com.

39. "Solar Power Applications in the Developing World," *Massachusetts Institute of Technology*, 2015. www.energy.mit.edu.

40. Quoted in Peter Reuell, "Bionic Leaf Turns Sunlight into Liquid Fuel," *Harvard Gazette*, June 2, 2016. www.news.harvard.edu.

41. "LEDS: Overview," *Solar Roadways*, 2016. www.solarroadways.com.

42. Quoted in Amanda Kolson Hurley, "Spray-On Solar Cells," *Johns Hopkins Health Review*, 2016. www.johnshopkinshealthreview.com.

43. "Space-Based Solar Power," *US Department of Energy*, March 6, 2014. www.energy.gov.

44. Quoted in Emmet Cole, "Space-Based Solar Farms Power Up," *BBC*, November 18, 2014. www.bbc.com.

45. "The Future of Solar Energy," *Massachusetts Institute of Technology*, 2015. www.energy.mit.edu.

BOOKS

John Allen, *Careers in Environmental and Energy Technology.* San Diego, CA: ReferencePoint, 2017.

Lester R. Brown, *The Great Transition: Shifting from Fossil Fuels to Solar and Wind Energy.* New York: W.W. Norton & Company, 2015.

Matt Doeden, *Green Energy: Crucial Gains or Economic Strains?* Minneapolis, MN: Twenty-First Century Books, 2010.

Stuart A. Kallen, *Cutting Edge Energy Technology.* San Diego, CA: ReferencePoint, 2017.

Andrea Nakaya, *What Is the Future of Solar Power?* San Diego, CA: ReferencePoint, 2012.

Christine Zuchora-Walske, *Solar Energy.* Minneapolis, MN: Abdo Publishing, 2013.

WEBSITES

Bureau of Labor Statistics: Careers in Solar Power
https://www.bls.gov/green/solar_power

On the website of the Bureau of Labor Statistics, the government agency that studies the nation's workforce, learn more about solar energy and the many careers that support this rapidly growing field.

Department of Energy: Solar
https://energy.gov/science-innovation/energy-sources/renewable-energy/solar

The website of the Department of Energy, the US agency that promotes innovative energy policies, features information about all kinds of renewable energy sources, including solar power.

New York Times: Solar Energy
https://www.nytimes.com/topic/subject/solar-energy

This link collects the latest stories about solar energy from the *New York Times*. Learn about the companies, scientists, engineers, and politicians who are shaping the future of solar power.

Solar Energy Industries Association
http://www.seia.org

The Solar Energy Industries Association (SEIA) is a trade group that advocates for the increased use of solar energy in the United States. Its comprehensive website includes news about the latest solar technologies, lists of US solar companies, and information about government policies related to solar power.

Solar Impulse
http://www.solarimpulse.com/adventure

The official website of the Solar Impulse project presents the story behind the historic around-the-world flight of *Solar Impulse 2*. Visitors can see pictures, watch videos, and read about the pilots, engineers, and technicians who made the voyage possible.

Solar Industry Magazine
http://solarindustrymag.com

The website of *Solar Industry* magazine features the latest updates on solar energy technologies and policies.

alternating current, 26
Arco Solar power plant, 27
artificial photosynthesis, 64–65

bandgap, 22–23
batteries, 26, 37, 38
Bell Labs, 19
birds, 42
Burj Khalifa, 17

China, 10, 27, 30, 36, 41, 69
climate change, 11, 34–36

Dawn spacecraft, 46–47
Department of Energy, US, 11, 17, 23, 25
direct current, 26

electrical grid, 37–39, 44, 63
electromagnetic spectrum, 21–22
Energy Information Administration, US, 30
energy storage, 20, 24, 26, 37, 38

fossil fuel problems, 10, 31–37
fossil fuels
coal, 29, 30, 31–32
diesel, 29
gasoline, 29
natural gas, 29–30
oil, 29, 30, 33

greenhouse effect, 34–35
greenhouse gases, 35

Helios Prototype, 52–53
hydroelectric power, 12, 44

India, 10, 27, 69
International Space Station, 48
Ivanpah Solar Plant, 18–19, 41–42

Japan, 69–70
jobs, 36–37
Juno spacecraft, 47–49

Massachusetts Institute of Technology, 10, 63, 71
Middle East, 37
multijunction solar cells, 22
Musk, Elon, 60–62

Nellis Air Force Base, 27
net metering, 38–40
nuclear fusion, 13–14
Nuna 8, 49–50

perovskite, 59–60
photons, 6, 13–14, 20, 21–23
photosynthesis, 12, 64, 65
photovoltaic cells
    applications, 24–27
    costs, 10
    efficiency, 22–24
    manufacturing, 40–41
    materials, 6, 20, 24–26
PlanetSolar, 56–57

quantum dots, 66

recombination, 23

SeaCharger, 55–56
silicon, 6–7, 19, 20, 22–24, 40–41,
    59–60, 66
Socrates, 14
Solar Impulse 2, 53–54
Solar Investment Tax Credit, 43
solar lanterns, 62–63
Solar One, 25
solar paint, 66
solar power
    costs, 37
    environmental challenges, 40–42
    history, 14, 19, 21, 24–25, 27
    policy challenges, 38–40
    tax exemptions, 43
    technical challenges, 37–38

Solar Roadways, 65–66
solar roofs, 61–62
Solar Star Projects, 7–9, 27
SolarHost program, 39
Space-based solar power, 67–69
Sun, 6, 12–14

thermal solar power
    concentrating collectors, 9–10,
        15–16, 18
    definition, 6, 9, 14
    efficiency, 17
    flat-plate collectors, 15
    molten salts, 16, 37
    solar water heating, 17
thin-film solar cells, 24, 41
Toyota solar Prius, 50–51

University of Delaware, 25

Vanguard 1 satellite, 45

Watt, James, 26, 29
wind power, 12, 44
World Solar Challenge, 50

ABOUT THE AUTHOR

Arnold Ringstad has written more than seventy books for readers ranging from kindergarteners to high schoolers. He has also published research in the *Journal of Cold War Studies*. Ringstad graduated from the University of Minnesota–Twin Cities in 2011. He lives in Minnesota with his wife and their cat.